# The
# Mighty Severn
# Bore

## Chris Witts

Cover & Chapter Illustrations
by
Nicki Witts

RIVER SEVERN PUBLICATIONS
GLOUCESTER   ENGLAND

First Published 1999
© Chris Witts 1999

ISBN 0 9532711 2 9


River Severn Publications
35 Lavington Drive
Gloucester
GL2 0HP

e-mail: chriswitts@ndirect.co.uk
www.severnbore.ndirect.co.uk




Typeset by
Protocol
Gloucester

Printed in England by
Icon Print & Design Ltd
Gloucester

# Contents

# Illustrations

## Photographs

## Drawings

Respect for a River

From Plynlimon you start your journey
Slowly, gently meandering south
Passing through so many counties
Finally to reach your mouth

You can adopt a human mantle
Sometimes giving sometimes taking
Endlessly progressing onwards
Tidal rhythms never breaking

On quieter days reflecting, soothing
Almost healing is your flow
Washing away man's pollution
Down the channel it will go

But when you're roused a different story
Brown mad fury, full of wrath
Sailors you have tossed asunder
Lost amongst the swirling froth

You possess fish in abundance
Rows of putchers - a dying art
In the springtime elvers travel
Miles from their Sargasso start

Oh Mighty Severn we may have bridged you
But your power remains untamed
Your wildness and freedom we envy
But your secrets stay unclaimed

Angela Moran
1996

# Preface

Higher above the Hafren Forest in Powys, 2,000 feet above
sea level in the wilds of Plynlimon rises Britain's longest
river, the Severn. Two Hundred and twenty miles later the mighty
Severn flows from the estuary into the Bristol Channel and eventually into the Atlantic Ocean. It is wild and desolate on the top of
Plynlimon where a trickle becomes a stream rapidly dropping down
the steep slopes as it enters the forest.

Tumbling over boulders, the water crystal clear, the Severn
continues to drop as it enters Llanidloes, then north onto Newtown,
passing the last Welsh town of Welshpool. As our planet was
formed all those millions of years ago the Severn continued to
travel north until it ran into the River Dee in Cheshire, but during
the last ice age a dramatic upheaval took place. The Severn above
Welshpool was dammed by massive boulders, Cheshire became
flooded and eventually the river altered course and ran south down
through England, passing through Shropshire, Worcestershire and
Gloucestershire before running into the Bristol Channel.

Since time began, twice a day, every day the tides have
risen up the Bristol Channel, continuing up the Severn Estuary to
Gloucester, [depending on the height of the tide, the smaller tides
only reach Newnham], with man taking full advantage of this mass
of water in the river. For centuries  men with their sailing craft
would sail up the Severn on the tide to Gloucester, they then had
the problem of getting their craft back down river again, for the tide

ebbed too fast to enable them to get from Gloucester to the Bristol Channel on one tide, it could even take three! For that reason the Gloucester and Sharpness Ship Canal was opened in 1827.

As we move into the 21st century the river has adopted a new image. With all commercial trade finished on the Severn, [except for the odd cargo of grain between Gloucester and Tewkesbury on the grain barges], the river is now only used for leisure activities and the supply of water for domestic and commercial use. Fishing as a hobby is not a new pastime and is as popular as ever. Private small craft on the river is nothing new either, but is now accessible to everyone and not just the rich. Hiring a narrow boat for a holiday break is a common pastime, especially between Tewkesbury and Stourport.

What is new is the sight of several surfers and canoeists riding the bore between Newnham and Gloucester. Of course not everyone is in favour of them pursuing this pastime on the Severn, some saying it spoils the spectacle of the bore. Maybe it does, but no one owns the Severn and the majority of surfers respect the river and if they don't, it is to their cost! Who would ever have thought that the world surfing record would be held by a Gloucester man and achieved by surfing the Severn.

The spring tides of the Severn not only effect the bore, but salmon and elvers to. These two fish are exact opposites of each other, the salmon swimming across the Atlantic to spawn high up the Severn and elvers moving en masse up river to grow into eels before returning to the Atlantic. The salmon will return to the Severn, the eel will not, once the female eel has spawned no one knows where she goes, only her off spring, the elver, make the long journey to our rivers.

The Severn Bore has given much pleasure to very many people each year, whether watching from the safety of the bank or surfing on the crest of the wave, hopefully, this will continue for many more years to come.

# The
# Severn Bore

T he twenty first century has almost arrived, bringing with it
the electronic age of computers, mobile phones, the Internet, all playing a major part in our lives and that of the River Severn too. When I telephoned London to register my URL address for
my website about the Severn, the young lady asked which name I
would like. I replied "severnbore", to which she answered, "but I'm
sure you are not a boring person!" So I then explained to her one of
nature's greatest free spectacles, the Severn Bore.

From all over the world I receive requests to supply infor-
mation about the bore, many from America who plan their holidays
to come to Gloucestershire to coincide when a good wave is forecast. Through the media of radio and newspapers good bores are
forecast and on the day  thousands line the banks below Gloucester,
yet on another day you may find that you are the only one present
with the river to yourself, free to enjoy this magical moment, which
after nearly fifty years of viewing the bore, it still makes the hairs
stand up on the back of my head, [the few that I have left!].

Our early ancestors, the Romans, on first sighting the bore
a little below Gloucester ran scared thinking the end of the world
was nigh! The name bore came from the Saxon word *bara*, a name
adopted by the tribal settlement of Hwicci, *men of the tidal creek.*
Yet in the 16th century the bore began to be called by another
name, *hygre,* used in fine prose by William Camden and Michael
Drayton. Local rivermen though preferred the original name of

bore, the term which we still use today. Reading their prose it paints a picture of a raging, boisterousness mass of water surging up the Severn, overflowing the banks and filling the land far inland with water. Overturning the toiling barge out in the river with the helmsman having fought a losing battle to keep his craft heading into the wave to avoid the turbulence.

Many people are disappointed by what they see, expecting a gigantic wave to surge up the river, higher than the bank! That has happened, as we shall see later, but very rare and only a few times in the last four hundred years. The surfers together with their high speed safety boats can be annoying, for part of the excitement of the bore is the sound it makes as it approaches and as it passes. Some say a good bore is rarely seen now due to the surfers continually breaking the crest of the wave as they ride it, stopping a large wave from forming.

To explain why the River Severn has a bore can be quite difficult. First it must be understood that the bore grows at a great distance from Gloucestershire, in fact in the mid Atlantic, travelling twice a day towards Europe due to the gravitational pull of the moon and to a lesser degree the sun. During the course of twelve months there are between 250 to 260 bores, or to put it another way, two bores a day for 130 days of the year. But when do they occur? They occur during that period known as spring tides, not spring as in the word to describe a season of the year, but as in *to leap up high*. A spring tide is the high tide that occurs once a fortnight to correspond with the full or new moon, the highest occurring during the Spring and Autumn equinoxes of March and September. A set of bores normally last between three and five days growing from a small one on the first day to a maximum on the middle and then declining. [*Fig 1*]

The Severn Estuary has the second highest rise and fall of tide in the world, the Bay of Fundy, Canada reputed to have the highest in the Petitcodial river. Between Beachley and Aust the difference between low and high water is 14.5m. At this location the river bed is lower than anywhere else in the Bristol Channel and Severn Estuary. From the Atlantic, into the Bristol Channel to-

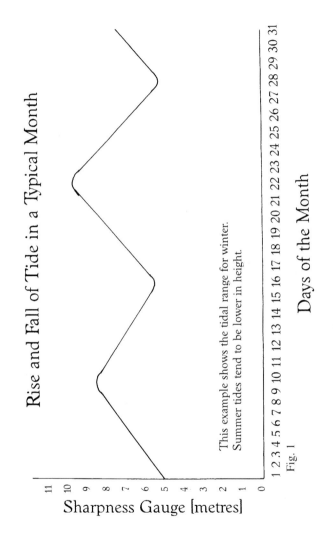

Rise and Fall of Tide in a Typical Month

Sharpness Gauge [metres]

11 10 9 8 7 6 5 4 3 2 1 0

This example shows the tidal range for winter.
Summer tides tend to be lower in height.

Fig. 1

1 2 3 4 5 6 7 8 9 10 11 12 13 14 15 16 17 18 19 20 21 22 23 24 25 26 27 28 29 30 31

Days of the Month

wards the Severn Estuary the sea bed is dropping away until at the Severn Suspension Bridge it begins to rise, continuing to rise all the way to the source.

As the tide races in from mid Atlantic it is travelling at great speed, but 200 miles off shore it reaches the continental shelf which slows down the flow, but increases the height. It then enters the Bristol Channel where its narrowing funnel shape has the effect of further increasing the height of this mass of water. When the tide enters the Severn its width has been narrowed from a hundred miles to less than five and the height increased by almost 15.2m. The force of water at the rear is driven on with less restriction and tries to overtake the forward part, add to the equation the rising river bed and the leading edge of the tide becoming unstable, then a wave is formed and we have our bore.

As the incoming tide enters the Severn Estuary at Avonmouth it is seen as a little wave barely 50mm high. Standing on the shore at Sharpness near the old dock entrance before the tide arrives large islands of sand banks can be seen, but soon these will be surrounded by a boiling mass of water. Slowly the sand disappears beneath the rapidly rising tide, a time to reflect that this is Britain's most dangerous river. Past Sharpness a wave begins to form, entering the long straight route to Awre, around the Noose only to crash into Hock Cliff at Fretherne. from this mass of confused water the bore reforms only to turn itself back down a seaward channel to collide with another incoming wave which has run up a channel formed on the opposite side of the sand banks. Again turmoil, but with the tide rising fast the reformed bore is soon running past Overton before swinging across the estuary towards Box Cliff, passing Newnham, Broadoak and Westbury on Severn. Back to the other side heading for Pridings, then clinging to the shore as it passes Framilode and Epney. At Framilode the tide has reached its maximum height above sea level, thus in effect this is where the tide stops, but its energy will push the mass of water as far as Tewkesbury.

Above Epney the river narrows, losing the feel of the sea and becoming an inland river where a little below Minsterworth the shape of the river is constant to Gloucester and is where the bore can be seen at its best. The wave is travelling at 15 mph and can build to a height of 2m.

A common question often asked of me is, "How can the tide be ebbing out at Sharpness, yet still flowing with force above Minsterworth towards Gloucester?". To explain this I use the example of someone throwing a cricket ball with a underhand movement. The ball is in the hand as the arm is drawn back behind the body, then very quickly the arm is brought forward and the ball let go, leaving the ball travelling forward at speed as the arm is being brought back. For this example relate the arm to the tide and the ball the bore. The late Fred Rowbotham used an example of a matchstick being shot from a toy gun, the spring shoots out the matchstick, whilst as the spring retracts the matchstick is still projected forward. This is the key element to the answer to your question, projection, the tide in the upper part of the Severn is projected to Gloucester and beyond.

It should be mentioned that quite a few of our rivers experience bores too, though the Severn is rated as being the most spectacular. The River Parrett in Somerset, which also flows into the Bristol Channel has them as does the River Trent, but here it is called an aegire.

# When to See the Bore

Tides come in fortnightly cycles with springs and neaps, where the spring is the highest of the cycle so the neap is the lowest, but the spring tide is highest in the equinox seasons of March and September and again the neap is at its lowest. Both the full moon and new moon play their part in these cycles over a twelve month period.

As mentioned earlier there are on average between 250 and 260 bores each year, that equates to two per day on about 130 days of the year. These figures do not include the 150 tides whereby the level of the river surges suddenly in the form of a long smooth wave, although crashing along the banks remaining smooth in mid-stream. Unlike the bore the flow doesn't reverse immediately, yet still gives the river an eerie feeling similar to that experienced with a good bore.

Normally any tide of 8m and over predicted at Sharpness will produce a watchable bore. How do you know when that is? J W Arrowsmith Ltd of Bristol produce an annual *Bristol Channel Tide Table* book which includes Sharpness and there is a section on Severn Bore predictions and times. Many shops along the Severn in Gloucestershire sell this tide table book. Alternatively a few web sites on the Internet, mine included, give times and predictions of the bore, just type in *River Severn* on the search engines and you will find a suitable site listed or go direct to mine at: *www. severnbore.ndirect.co.uk.*

Having found a suitable day for your trip to the Severn to view the bore, it is then necessary to calculate when it will arrive at your vantage point, the table below will help. It goes without saying that a good map is essential, preferably an ordnance survey map.

## TIME DIFFERENCE CALCULATIONS
### Based on High Water at Sharpness

| | |
|---|---|
| Maisemore Bridge | add 40 mins. |
| Over Bridge | add 35 mins. |
| Lower Parting | add 33 mins. |
| Upper Rea, Hempsted | add 20 mins. |
| Stonebench | add 15 mins. |
| Elmore Back | High Water @ Sharpness |
| Minsterworth | High Water @ Sharpness |
| Severn Bore Inn | subtract 3 mins. |
| Epney | subtract 20 mins. |
| Framilode | subtract 25 mins. |
| Westbury Strand | subtract 45 mins. |
| Broadoak | subtract 50 mins. |
| Newnham | subtract 60 mins. |
| Bullo Pill | subtract 67 mins. |
| The Hock | subtract 85 mins. |
| Awre | subtract 90 mins. |

# Nature and the Bore

Although the bore is quite predictable on its time of arrival at your chosen location several factors dictate the height of the tide.

## Bore will arrive Later if:

Strong north to east winds
No freshwater in river
Bore cutting a longer channel through estuary sands
High barometer reading

## Bore will arrive Earlier if:

Strong south to south-west winds
Up to 15m of freshwater in river
Bore cutting shorter channel through estuary sands
Low barometer reading

## Bore height Smaller if:

Strong north to east winds
No freshwater in river
Too much freshwater in river
High barometer reading

## Bore height Increased if:

Strong west to south-west winds
0.75m of freshwater in river below Gloucester
Channels through estuary sand well scoured
Low barometer reading

*Note:* *The term 'freshwater' refers to the amount of water in the river above normal seasonal level. After a spell of rain farther up the river the level of the Severn will rise.*

The famous photograph of the bore at Lower Parting taken in 1921

*from a postcard*

# Where to See the Bore

The best place to see the bore is not really the safest or most practical spot to be when a big wave is forecast! Stonebench offers the best view of a good bore, but the tide can come over the bank here, making it dangerous for you and may also fill your car with water, also Stonebench is located on a narrow lane system which causes traffic chaos, necessitating the local police to enforce a temporary one way system.

I favour Minsterworth on the opposite bank, approached from the A48 with good access to the river bank adjacent to the church. [*Fig 2*] For the first time bore watcher an ideal spot, safe from the tides, but offering a good view of the bore. Should you wish to avoid the crowds arrive early at Minsterworth and walk against the flow of the current towards Gloucester, using the public footpath along the river bank, where eventually you will reach a spot opposite Stonebench after a leisurely twenty minute walk.

# THE RIVER SEVERN
# AT GLOUCESTER

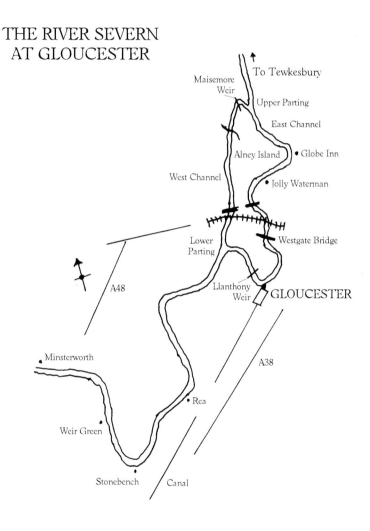

Fig. 2

It was possible not so many years ago to see the bore lower down the river, jump in the car to travel further on to see the bore again and repeat this several times before seeing the bore as it stops and rises above Maisemore Weir at Gloucester. [*Fig 3*] Sadly with the heavy volume of traffic now on our roads and the difficulty in finding somewhere to park, this can no longer be done, especially on a weekend when a good bore is forecast, the crowds are phenomenal.

As mentioned previously the typical media hyped bore is best seen between Minsterworth and Gloucester, but further down the river towards the estuary the tide coming in can be just as exciting. Though the best places are again the most difficult to get to, Hock Cliff at Fretherne is such a place, the footpath is well sign posted, it is finding somewhere to park the car that can be difficult!

The golden rule of bore watching is to arrive early, time and tide waits for no man, especially the bore. More often than not the bore arrives late, but you can guarantee on the day you arrive late the bore will have been early! Don't climb down the bank to the waters edge as you will not have time to climb back up to safety once the bore arrives. Remember it isn't just the wave which is unique, the river fills to bank high in a few minutes with all that mass of water following the bore, plus carrying along with it, whole trees uprooted further down and numerous other forms of waste.

You may be lucky and have the river to yourself with no other form of man made noise to spoil it, then suddenly you will hear a noise likened to an express train approaching, a gentle breeze picks up and then around the bend the wave can be seen. Crashing along the bank, picking up any loose debris in its path, the excitement is in the air as it gets closer, the noise now very loud and then it is passing by, a boiling, frothy mass of water. As quick as it approached, it is gone, eyes gaze upriver as it disappears around the bend, but stay patient, don't rush off back to the car, stay awhile to watch the river rapidly filling up with water as the current races by. Quieter now, but just as spectacular with such a force of water still racing by towards Gloucester. Hard to imagine

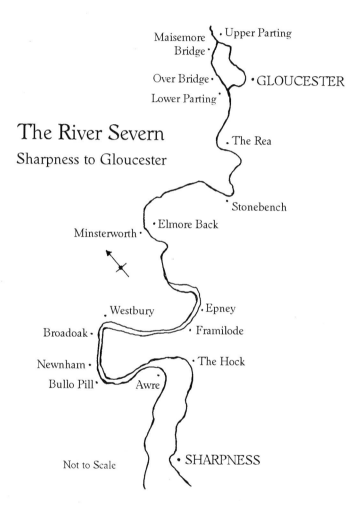

The River Severn

Sharpness to Gloucester

Fig. 3

that now the tide is ebbing out at Sharpness! If your patience will last, wait an hour, have another cup of hot coffee from that flask you remembered to bring, for as the tide begins to turn everything becomes still and quiet. Birds fall silent, the wind drops as the tide, first on each side of the bank then the middle, stops, the flow reverses, taking all that mass of water back to the sea.

Was it a good bore? For me every bore is a good one. To think that not so many years ago plans were made to construct a barrage across the estuary to harness this mass of water for generating power. That would have destroyed one of nature's best free treasures, the mighty Severn Bore.

Dramatic view of the bore as it races towards Gloucester

*Patricia Larkham*

# The Bore above Gloucester

Officially, most agree that the Severn Bore terminates at Gloucester, but that is not always the case. For the tide to rise over the two weirs at Gloucester, the tide must reach 8m minimum on the Sharpness Pier gauge. Obviously the higher the tide over 8m at Sharpness the greater the volume of water surging over the weirs.

The Severn was canalised during the mid 19th century by building a series of locks and weirs between Gloucester and Stourport to guarantee craft enough water in the river to trade into the Midlands. Prior to this, barges and trows traded far up the Severn over the Shropshire border into a little place below the Welsh market town of Welshpool called Pool Quay. It could take weeks for the crews of these vessels to get their craft from Gloucester up the shallow river to Pool Quay and the same amount of time to come back down! Their only hope of an easy passage were the large spring tides that would pass Gloucester before gradually dying, but holding the normal river flow in check causing a rise in river level.

After a period of rain, especially up in the Welsh hills, the level of the Severn will rise very quickly, helped also by the numerous tributaries running into the river. This *freshwater,* as any level above normal summer level is termed, would have given the barges and trows a quick passage downstream to Gloucester, some travelling down from Shropshire to Gloucester in less than 24 hours!

Four weirs now effect the running of the bore, Maisemore and Llanthony at Gloucester, Upper Lode at Tewkesbury and Diglis at Worcester. On an average spring tide it will rise over Upper Lode weir and reverse the flow for about a mile upstream to where the River Avon joins the Severn, a large tide though, will cause the river level to rise by up to 50mm as far inland as Worcester.

At Gloucester there is a large island known as Alney Island, surrounded on all sides by the River Severn, one channel is named the West Channel and is the shorter of the two, the other is the East Channel, also called The Parting, which is the navigational channel. The split in the Severn is below Gloucester and as the tide surges up the river the majority of the flow continues up the West Channel until it reaches Maisemore weir where it stops before rising over the weir to continue on to where the two channels join again. Meanwhile some of the tide has entered the East Channel rising over Llanthony weir and continuing past Gloucester Lock, along The Quay towards the Upper Parting some three miles away.

The tide in the West Channel has reached the Upper Parting long before that running up the other leg of the river, The main force of the flow will continue upriver towards Tewkesbury, but some will flow down into the East Channel where at the Globe Inn it meets up again with the confused tide running up from Gloucester. The current stops both ways for a moment before the more powerful tide from Gloucester is forcing back the weaker current and soon the whole flow is making back upstream to join the main tide above the Upper Parting.

The bore as it swings into the East Channel of The Parting.
*Chris Witts*

# On the Bore

Many years ago my brother gave me an old cine camera for my birthday, so armed with plenty of film I set off for Elmore to film the bore. It must have been beginners luck for I captured a good bore with Fred Rowbotham on his barge, the RIPARIAN, riding the wave. Later he told me what it was like to be on a large vessel waiting out in the river for a predicted good bore.

"Not for the feint hearted and not my favourite vessel to be riding the bore with", he told me, "that is a good stout rowboat with a good pair of oars". Whether waiting on the Severn to ride the bore with a rowing boat or a motor barge, the principal is the same. Make sure there is sufficient deep water under the barge and try to be on a straight reach so as to give yourself plenty of warning of the approaching bore. Fred lived for excitement and if he felt one side of the river had a low unexciting wave he would move over to the other side hopefully where there would be a high wave.

Waiting out in the river for the bore to appear can feel like a lifetime, especially with the nerve tingling butterflies in the stomach. Wait you must, but only in the middle of the river and facing in the direction that the bore will come from. This is the problem for how do you keep a vessel stationary whilst the normal river current will be taking you downstream? To anchor the boat or to tie it up to a tree on the bank would be inviting disaster.

As the bore approaches the mind races from decision to decision, stay in the middle to face it head on, move to the side to meet a high point, whatever, it has to be ridden now as it is almost upon you! Boat and wave meet with the wave stopping the boat so requiring a few extra revs on the engine or an extra pull on the oars to stop you going backwards. But then you still have to face the second, third and fourth waves, fortunately decreasing in height as you ride over them, into troughs and up the other side.

Within a minute the excitement is over then the anticlimax as your body feels exhausted and flat. No time to rest though, for the river is rapidly filling with all that powerful mass of water following behind the bore. Travelling with such force it is a job to keep the barge stemming the flow to maintain steerage. To try to turn the vessel around and run with the flow would be foolhardy as there would be a good chance that the barge would be taken sideways up the river and out of control.

Not so long ago a family visiting Lydney for the first time asked the advice of a local resident on how safe it would be to take their inflatable boat out on the Severn. The advice given was stupid and nearly cost the lives of this young family of husband, wife and three young children.

Full of confidence following the assurance that it would be okay to be out on the Severn in their small boat they launched the inflatable below Newnham to set off upriver. As they passed the toilet block above Newnham the boat hit the notorious rock which is known to all experienced men who sail the Severn. Unfortunately for our foolhardy family the bore was quickly upon them and as it hit the stricken boat threw it up in the air, overturned it and tossed the family into the river.

Luckily for them they had taken the precaution of wearing life jackets and were able to cling to the upturned boat as it sped fast up the Severn with the tide. Unbelievable they travelled like this for many miles until when passing Framilode and Epney on the opposite bank a Severnsider saw their predicament and was able to go out into the river and rescue them.

It cannot be emphasised enough, the River Severn is a very dangerous river to be on below Gloucester, especially when the large spring tides are running. Only a handful of men know the river well enough to be able to safely take a boat on it. The best advice is, stay off the river unless accompanied by one of these men.

A truly mighty Severn Bore as it races towards Gloucester.
*courtesy of Gloucester Folk Museum*

People on the bank and surfers both enjoy the bore as it passes Minsterworth
*Patricia Larkham*

# Living on the Bore

Can you imagine being prepared for your home to take a severe battering from the elements during the cold winter months of winter, watching a wave of water coming towards you at 15 mph? Mike and Susan May and their family do just that each month. Why? Because they live on the bore!

Two years ago Mike bought an old converted river barge, the WILCLAIR, from where he saw her lying forlorn on the mud at Chepstow. Previous to that she had lain at Bristol as a floating restaurant, but her history goes back a long way. Built in 1935 by the now defunct yard of Charles Hill at Bristol she was named SEVERN INDUSTRY and traded on the Severn between Avonmouth and Stourport carrying general cargo, from aluminium ingots to cans of baked beans.

Mike had bought some land at Stonebench, which included the derelict Stonebench Inn, built to serve the needs of the crew of sailing ships which used to moor here whilst waiting for sufficient water to get them to Gloucester until it finally closed its doors and ceased to be a pub in 1948. First he had to prepare a berth for the WILCLAIR at the side of the bank including a strong anchorage with which to moor the barge to. After this it was time to bring the barge up the Severn to Stonebench under her own power as fortunately the engine was still in working order. Today as you stand and gaze at this remarkable sight of a lime green painted barge moored snugly on her berth with an attractive decorative brick topped jetty it is difficult to imagine the hard graft it has taken to achieve this. Photographs and video tell the story of the sea of mud on the shore following the floods, the problems of access to their home, added to by remembering that Mike and Susan have young children too. The constant worry of making sure they didn't fall in the river.

As if this wasn't enough, they still had the worry of what the bore would do to the barge as it came surging up the river. Remember they are at Stonebench, one of the best places to see a good bore on the Severn.

The WILCLAIR laying on her berth at Stonebench.

*Mike May collection*

The WILCLAIR as she is struck by the bore

*courtesy of The Citizen*
*Gloucester*

In the early days it was a bit of a worry for Mike as he would watch the approaching wave then hear the sickening thud as it hit the barge sending a plume of spray high in the air. For a further twenty minutes the water level rises up the side of the barge sufficiently to float her, [before the bore arrives the vessel is sitting on the mud] creating a creaking sound from the hull as pressure is applied from the incoming tide which can be quite frightening. Nowadays Mike is used to it, but admits to being a little apprehensive in the beginning. As an extra precaution he increases the number of mooring ropes from barge to shore during the big spring tides. Even then he still makes sure the engine is ready for a quick start just in case the WILCLAIR should break free from her moorings and drift out into the river.

More often than not the bore will arrive late, but Susan well remembers the day when it arrived forty minutes early! Shouting to Mike, they couldn't believe their eyes as the bore raced towards them. The river had some fresh water flowing down as well as a south westerly gale blowing up the river behind the tide, a good combination for a big bore. It was an awesome sight to see the bore coming straight for them whilst at the same time running over the fields on the opposite bank! As you can imagine Mike May has seen many bores in his time, more than most and this one was something extraordinary.

Mike and his family will not be living on the barge for much longer as they are building a new home a little way further along the bank. They will be sad to move out of their present home for not only is it cosy and warm, but the view from the saloon window overlooking the Severn is stunning. One thing for sure he doesn't plan to sell her or move her, he is too fond of her now and wishes to enjoy the fruits of two years of hard labour in what he toiled and sweated assisted by family and friends in achieving this unique home.

The WILCLAIR is not the only vessel Mike owns, he has another barge, the ARRETON, which he used for contract work between Swansea and Gloucester. Now sadly with the high cost of insurance he has laid her up in a field at The Rea. A barge in a field! The ARRETON, in late 1998 was moved on the highest tide of the year from Stonebench to The Rea, driven ashore where she remains high and dry, a strange sight, but safe. This vessel was built at Newcastle-upon Tyne and it had been planned to send her to the Dardanelles during the First World War.

Like all Severnsiders, Mike loves the river and uses it not just for his home, but leisure pursuits as well. When time permits he enjoys being out on a big tide with his 4m Avon SeaRider inflatable, assisting Dave Lawson as he surfs for a new record. He wants as many people as possible to enjoy the river, but warns, take care, the Severn is there to catch out the unwary.

The Severn Bore passing Stonebench Inn

*from a postcard*

Today, seventy years after this photograph was taken, all that remains of the Inn is just the derelict shell of the building.
Now beyond any hope of restoration, no doubt it will not be too long before it has to be demolished.

# Flood of 1606

Nature has a way of keeping us in our place, fortunately in the UK we must be behaving ourselves as we suffer relatively few natural disasters.. Earthquakes, tornadoes and volcanoes are problems associated with other parts of the world, disasters we discuss over a pint down at our local. Sympathy shown to those who suffer, but the subject soon forgotten.

Perhaps we shouldn't be so complacent though. We, as an island nation are surrounded by the sea and the fear of a tidal wave is maybe something we should not treat as a fictional horror story.

On the 20th January 1606 the men and women of the small hamlets along the banks of the Severn Estuary were preparing to go about their daily tasks, with some no doubt having discussed already the high tide of the night before. Owing to a strong gale blowing up the Bristol Channel the height of the tide had been considerable higher than predicted. Perhaps the locals should have been prepared for what was about to happen that fateful Tuesday morning!

As they awoke from their sleep they were greeted by a wet and windy day, but the work still had to be done so it is doubtful whether many gave a thought to the fact that today was forecast as having the highest tide of the year on the Severn with conditions right for a good bore. With lack of the luxury of our modern communication network they would not have known how much danger they were shortly to be in.

Without warning salt water to a depth of 2m swept across land both sides of the Severn Estuary. It was running through the windows on one side of the houses and out through windows on the other. Men, women and children perished in the flood. Hundreds of cattle and horses drowned, whilst thousands of sheep and lambs were lost. Many rich people in the morning were beggars by the afternoon!

Some of the people in their houses climbed onto the high beams, others clambered out through open windows onto the roofs, all waiting to be rescued by boats sent from afar as Bristol. A few even built rafts from the windows to escape to higher ground.

For five hours the deluge ran over the banks covering an area for a distance of six miles inland, with the strange sight of carcasses of wild animals including foxes, rabbits and rats floating together with dead people and cattle.

A report written by John Pawle, the vicar of Almondsbury on the 26th January 1606 stated that a tidal wave had swept up the Bristol Channel from Minehead to Slimbridge which had affected not just the Severn, but the Wye, Avon and Monow. Much damage was done in Saul and Fretherne with the flood water lying on the land for a further five days, much to the annoyance of the local vicar.

Could it happen again? Yes, for this is only one incident of several that have been recorded, the most recent being the terrible east coast floods during the mid twentieth century.

The Mighty Severn Bore

# Surfing
# The Severn

Surfing the River Severn doesn't have the same ring to it as surfing on the West Coast of California. Yet the world wave riding record is held by a Gloucestershire man and it was achieved on the Severn! Surfing conjures up visions of the Beach Boys singing their famous song *Surfin' USA*, the sunny, blue skies of California and Bondi Beach in Australia with tanned male idols riding the surf. A lot different scene to that on the Severn on a cold, grey winters day with several men in wet suits out on their boards surfing the bore!

## Dave Lawson and His Record

Dave Lawson at fifty two years old holds the world wave riding record. Inspired as long ago when a teenager he saw two Australian lifeguards surfing the bore on the Severn and thought he would like to do that one day. But first he realised he would have to master the art of surfing so he began by travelling down to Croyde Bay in Devon and Porthcawl in Wales to surf in the sea in the conventional way.

He has lived alongside the Severn for most of his life, as a lad at Stonebench and now in a farmhouse at The Rea, Gloucester. Never one to be frightened of water he recalls as a young boy of hearing a crowd of people on the bank opposite Stonebench shouting that there was a sheep in the river. Knowing that the bore was due any minute he gallantly jumped into the Severn and pulled the sheep into the bank. With all the effort he could muster he pushed the heavily water laden animal up the bank just as the bore came sweeping around the bend. Like all good Severn men, Dave as a young man got himself a job as deckhand on the infamous John Harker tanker barges which operated from Swansea to Worcester on the Severn in the 1950s and 60s.

It wasn't until he was twenty-eight years old that he felt he had the confidence and knowledge to surf the Severn Bore. Even then he knew he had a lot to learn so used to belly ride his board until he mastered the art of being able to stand on the board to ride the wave. Over the years Dave has developed his own distinctive technique of standing on the board and is sure that it is this stance which helped him obtain the world record. In those early days Dave would be alone and with his car would drive to a spot along the river, jump in the Severn, surf the bore for a short distance, get out, move the car and do the same again, several times until his stamina ran out. Even now he will wait in the river with his board for the bore to reach his house, intending only to ride the wave for a short distance, then find himself at Maisemore Weir where he has to telephone his wife for her to come and collect him!

The River Severn below Gloucester has always been recognised as a dangerous river. especially during spring tides, therefore Dave Lawson treats it with respect. He didn't expect to be able to drop his board in the water, get on it and surf the bore like an old hand. It took a very long time of practise, practise, practise, persevering until he was able to, at least, stand on his board and surf a short distance.

His one fear whilst surfing the bore is being thrown by the wave into the bank. The wave will roll you over and over for at least a dozen times before letting you go and during that time being bruised and battered from hitting the bank. Imagine if you should strike some debris or at worst bang your head on a tree stump or rocks, at best you would be knocked out, at worst killed! Dave has been thrown into the bank to be tossed around, but instead of climbing up the bank for safety he says this is the worst thing to do,

Dave Lawson silhouetted against the spray of the bore. Note the distinctive style of how he holds his hands.

*Dave Lawson collection*

swim out into middle of the river, there is safety in the water. One time he recalls being pinned against a tree whilst remaining upright, the pressure from the water was enormous, but don't panic for in a few seconds the river will let go.

Not everyone is in favour of the surfers surfing the bore. Those against the surfers being on the river whilst the bore is running says it spoils their view of it and doesn't give the wave chance to build into a big one. Dave has had large pebbles thrown from the bank at him!

Dave Lawson is very philosophical about the Severn and says the river is here for everyone to enjoy. He is the first man to offer guidance and assistance to anyone not sure of the best way of doing things, of course not everyone takes his advice.

The world record came to the Severn in 1988 when Dave reached a distance of 2.7 miles, but eight years later this was broken by his friend and rival Steve King from Saul who more than doubled it. Then on the Thursday morning tide of 29th August 1996 Dave put his board into the river at Weir Green and rode the crest of the wave for 5.7 miles beating Steve's short lived record by a fifth of a mile. He was sometimes nervous and almost lost it a couple of times, but he stayed on his board for almost 40 minutes, crossing bank to bank six times.

When attempting a record like this he has to put a lot of planning in to it. The British Surfing Association has to send an official adjudicator who will log it before it can go in the record books. Dave insists on a rescue boat in the form of an inflatable with a powerful outboard engine to follow him, usually crewed by his stepson Shaun. He can't see the record being broken on the Severn again, he thinks Weir Green to Maisemore Weir is the longest distance the wave travels without breaking up. Of course if he could find sponsors he would like an attempt on the bore of the Yangtze River in China. Waves there have been known to travel for up to 50 miles!

It is not only surfers who ride the bore, canoeists can be seen on the crest of the wave. Dave Lawson has twice rescued canoeists when their canoes have overturned trapping them underneath. On one occasion he was surfing the bore when he glanced sideways to see a canoe roll over without righting itself, but worse, the occupant never appeared on the surface. Dave abandoned his surfing and fought his way over to where the canoe was stuck on the bank. With a lot of difficulty he managed to get the man to the surface.

All the regular surfers of the Severn Bore agree on one thing, the river is dangerous and to seek advice from them before attempting to ride the wave. Never attempt it without a back-up boat following behind.

Posing for the camera as the high speed inflatable rescue boat passes Stonebench.

*Mike May collection*

37

# The River Severn Bore Riders Club

Inspired by tales of Colonel Churchill a group of enthusiastic surfers decided to form the River Severn Bore Riders Club in September 1998.

Colonel Churchill at 10.30am on the 21st July swam out into the Severn from the bank below Stonebench with his surfboard to wait for the predicted good bore. He was not disappointed for the 9.5m tide at Sharpness produced a fair sized bore and as it approached Churchill he placed his board beneath him and started to swim upstream. Soon the leading slope of the bore was beneath him and he began to plane forward using deft leg movements and balance to control his movement on the board.

His plan and hopes were to ride the bore for miles, but all that was dashed as he ran into shallower water at Stonebench causing the wave to break and throw the Colonel off his board. He had to struggle with his surfboard through the boiling water of the confusing river which follows the bore's aftermath. Disappointed that he had not travelled far, but determined to try again the following year.

Following years did see more skilled surfers on the Severn, Rodney Sumpter in 1967 managed a good ride, as did a team from the AA magazine, Drive, who in 1970 rode the bore for two miles. From far and wide they come to ride the bore, with Australian surfers, [as one would expect], having reasonable success.

To the casual observer on the shore the bore passes so quickly that it is difficult to study the formation of the wave, but for surfers it is a different story. They each have studied it, discussed it and are still exploring possibilities of finding other surfing channels downstream of Awre. New terms of describing the wave can be heard, a *jacking wave*, one which will usually fall over and peel from the peak, *barrelling* left or right, or for it to *barrel* out into the centre of the river from the bank.

Only on the bore wave can a surfer get a ride. Uncommon, but it does sometimes happen when the bore wave collapses, the following trough may work itself into a wave adequate to surf on.

Obviously if conditions are right and a good bore is predicted then the surfers should enjoy a good ride, finding a ridable wave anywhere between Awre and Maisemore weir, a distance of 23 miles. But for them the best is above the Severn Bore public house where the river is narrow and waves of 1.6m in the middle and 2.5m at the bank edges can be experienced.

It can't be emphasised enough that very proficient surfers ride the bore well, but it is no place for a novice on their own, the Severn is one of our most dangerous rivers. The most suitable board for surfing the Severn is the *longboard*, specified as being over 2.8m in length, but ideally the longer the better, 3.4m to 4.0m being the best to catch and stand up for long distances. Some *boogie ride* the Severn, [I did say we were taking the Severn and her bore into the 21st century!], on a *bodyboard*. A small light board that acts as a buoyancy aid as the surfing adopts the prone position, [lying down], and are great for white water riding on the river over long distances.

For those of you with access to the Internet, the River Severn Bore Riders Club has an excellent web site at: *http://members. tripod.com/~BoreRidersClub/index.html*

Reproduced below is an excerpt from their diary page:
*September 7th - 10th*
*Matt and I had an early start at 'The Severn Bore' for this months session and the reputation of the bore was immediate as we met up with a group of travelling Germans who had specifically stopped in England to ride the bore before heading on to surf the Irish coasts. The first day saw some good rides by a couple of the guys - Marcus headed a long way around the bend at the pub and ended up getting out on the opposite side to his camper leaving him stranded for quite a while. While Oli got a good mile ride at Over, and several of us rode from just above the Parting to the bridge. It's so wicked as a whole array of cars and campers speed up the A48 from spot to spot to get there before the wave, then burning through fields and sliding down the mud banks - quite an experience!*

*On the second day, Matt and Oli rode a good mile and half from below Over right up to the weir itself where the bore is finally forced to back up in its course. Disaster nearly struck as they both had to dive for the bank and clutch at trees to narrowly avoid being dragged into the weir! Matt repeated this on the Thursday but was fortunately given a lift out by Dave Lawson's speed boat.*

*Once again the river was fairly empty over the period except for the occasional canoeist and a couple of the local guys turned up. It was cool meeting the German crew and seeing them all so stoked after the first day that they ended up staying longer than planned.*

*Reproduced with permission from*
*Tomo Wright of the Bore Riders Club*

The River Severn Bore Riders Club is still fairly small, but it is not a male only domain, there are a couple of young ladies who surf the bore, risking with the men the dangers and the thrills. They are very helpful to other aspiring Severn surf-riders in that they will offer good advice to anyone contemplating going out on the bore for the first time. Full details of their club and contacts can be found on their web site.

Top British professional longboarder "Guts" Griffiths occasionally rides the bore with members of the club and is eager to have another stab at Lawson's world record in the near future. Surfers on the Severn may have their critics who say they are spoiling the fun for others who come to watch the bore from the bank. But is it that different now to the days of Fred Rowbotham when you would see him frequently riding the bore with his large barge accompanied by an even larger Regent tanker barge!

They make it look so easy! Surfing the Severn on a good bore wave.
*Patricia Larkham*

# Severn
# Tugs & Barges

The first powered vessels trading on the Severn were a fleet of steam tugs which would pull a string of lighters, barges, the trows and even narrow boats, [or longboats as they are called on the Severn], from Bristol and Avonmouth up the Severn Estuary to Sharpness. From Sharpness they would travel 16 miles along the Gloucester and Sharpness Ship Canal before locking out into the Severn at Gloucester, from where they could trade as far as Stourport, with the longboats travelling on far into the Midlands along the narrow canal system. Then came the motor barges, which reached a peak in the 1950s and 60s with the large fleet of tanker barges carrying petroleum products into Worcester and Stourport. These large barges would have loaded 350 tonnes of petrol at Swansea, the Welsh port at the mouth of the Bristol Channel. A most inhospitable place to be especially with a south west gale blowing, tossed around like a toy boat in a bath, the crew of four men glad when they docked at Sharpness, safe after taking a battering from the mountainous waves. Their troubles weren't over though, they still had to struggle to get the deeply laden craft up the shallow river to Worcester, on a good day taking seven hours from Gloucester, a journey which today will take 30 minutes in a car! It was a blessing therefore when they knew a large tide was due for this would reduce the time it took to get to Worcester by a few hours.

Sadly all this trade finished when the motorways were opened and a huge pipeline ran oil products into the Midlands near

Birmingham during the 1970s, leaving only two grain barges trading on the Severn. [At the time of writing this they to are laid up at Tewkesbury].

Men working on the Severn weren't known for their writing skills, thus it is only by reading the works of historian Hugh Conway-Jones as in his book *"Working Life on the Severn & Canal"* that a true picture emerges of the problems encountered by men on the river during the early part of the century. As there is no one alive who worked on the trows during the 18th & 19th centuries we have to imagine how difficult it must have been for them, especially as their craft had no engines! One thing is known, the East Channel of The Parting between Gloucester and Sandhurst was very different to how it looks today. By studying old photographs taken near Westgate Bridge the river looked idyllic with pleasure boats moored to the bank, people enjoying themselves and few trees crowding the banks. What a different picture today with the area in a sad decline, the river looking inhospitable , too many trees overhanging the banks, not the place to leave boats moored anymore.

As skipper of the last commercial barges to work on the Severn I was often asked if I had any qualifications or masters ticket. None, I replied, but plenty of common sense and knowledge of the river learnt as a lad on the tanker barges and as mate with Lionel Langford on the grain barges. A mate became eligible to be a skipper when the master of the vessel said so, no other word counted, his word was law. So as I relate tales of the difficulties encountered by bargemen in the past and later when you read of my stories of how I struggled with the grain barges, you will see how little the working conditions have changed.

Every trip on the Severn above Gloucester was different, the crew knew this and were always ready to think fast to get themselves out of trouble. As steam tugs were introduced so they were met with a fresh set of problems, for they not only had themselves to look after, but the men and craft strung behind the tug, connected together by single ropes, from craft to craft. Tug skippers knew when the big tides were due and planned their trip accordingly. At Gloucester if the tide was due shortly after they had locked down into the Severn all the craft would moor to The Quay until the first of the tide has gone by. The tug would then ease ahead until all the tow ropes were tight then the last barge would let go their mooring rope and then it was full speed ahead to race up The Parting with the flow.

If the tide was not due until later and the tug and tow were almost to the end of The Parting the skipper would ease down on the revs and wait for the first of the tide to pass across the entrance of the east channel as it swept up from Maisemore. As we noted earlier some of the water enters the east channel with quite a force which would stop the tug and her tow requiring all the revs the engineer could muster to stem the flow and slowly edge out into the main channel above Sandhurst. Once in the fast flowing current it was full speed up as far as Haw Bridge and beyond. Most tug skippers would not leave the East Channel of The Parting until the tide had arrived, but of course some would, taking a chance and hoping the tide didn't arrive early! Why? Because with all the turmoil of tide against the normal current flowing down, the water is in a confused state which would wash the barges all over the place.

Likewise when coming down river to Gloucester it was timed so that they didn't meet the first of the tide at The Parting. Soon after passing Ashleworth the revs on the tug were eased back and a careful eye kept open for the arrival of the tide. A tug going too fast and towing a loaded barge would force the towed craft under the water as it hit the tide causing it to sink. The tide surges up the reach between The Parting and Ashleworth with such force that as soon as the tug met it and after all the tow ropes tightened then the revs were increased to full speed just to maintain steerage against the strong current. Then another set of problems met them, for as the tide turns and ebbs out so the force of the current increases back to Gloucester and to maintain steerage with the tow behind the tug, their craft has to match that of the current, which is frightening as you negotiate the sharp, tight bends in The Parting!

# The Grain Barges

An earlier mention was made of the numerous motor barges that traded upriver above Gloucester during the 1950s and 60s, but from that period to the present day the River Severn has changed dramatically, with large trees lining the banks along the course of The Parting, overhanging into the river, the bed of the river is heavily silted, resulting in lack of depth of water. It used to be possible for two large tanker barges to pass each other in The Parting, now the navigational channel is too narrow for that!

For eight years prior to 1993 no commercial barges traded on the Severn above Gloucester, then in that year Allied Mills Limited of Tewkesbury began using their two grain barges again, with each barge, the CHACELEY and TIRLEY, loading 250 tonnes of grain at Sharpness for delivery to their flour mill located a short distance up the River Avon at Tewkesbury. Skipper of the TIRLEY since 1972 from when the barge first appeared on the Severn until her lay-up in 1985 Lionel Langford was once again asked to be master of the two grain barges. Working on the Severn since leaving school at fourteen years of age there wasn't much Lionel didn't know about the navigational part of the river between Avonmouth and Stourport, beginning his working life on the steam tugs, progressing to the modern tanker barges before finishing his career with the grain trade. For myself 1993 was to be a new era in my life when late one night I received a telephone call from Lionel asking me to go as his mate on the two grain barges.

I jumped at the chance and spent a couple of years learning as much as I could about the Severn between Gloucester and Tewkesbury. Lionel was a good teacher as well as telling some gripping tales of life on the river as a young lad on the tugs. Through these tales I was able to put together in my mind the safe places to be with the barge and the areas where if I drifted out of the channel we may come to grief with the vessel. As the navigational part of the river is so murky it is hard to imagine that beneath the surface lie many obstacles, mud banks, shallow water, boulders, trees lying stuck in the mud, all to be avoided, or else! Each bend presented its own problems, the current of the river varies considerably from reach to reach, get it wrong coming down The Parting empty and control of the barge is lost, as I found out to my cost, on several occasions! Even Lionel found when we first began running again in 1993, how much the river had changed and commented that it was more difficult to take a barge from Gloucester to Tewkesbury then than only eight years previously. Sadly Lionel died in 1995 and I was appointed skipper until once again the barges' were laid up at Tewkesbury in 1998.

It was to be a difficult five years battling to get the barges' up the Severn above Gloucester, getting stuck in the silt on numerous occasions. We would look forward to a good spring tide to assist us upriver to Tewkesbury, but that had its disadvantages as well, for the higher the tide, the greater the ebb is, with a strong current as it runs down The Parting, taking a few days following the spring tides to settle back down to a more leisurely flow. With the added problem of a shallow river and barges' with poor power it could take hours to navigate the three miles from Gloucester to the top of The Parting.

Arrowsmith's Bristol Channel Tide Book was consulted regularly to work out the best time to be in The Parting during the spring tides where I would aim to be midway between the Jolly Waterman, [a large house about 1 mile downstream from the Globe Inn], and the Globe Inn with the laden barge and her 250 tonne cargo of grain. With this amount of grain in the hold the barge has 2.1m of hull under the water and in places the river would normally only be 1.6m deep at low summer level! The first indication that the tide has arrived is when the bow, 37m away from where I am in the wheelhouse, dips to the river bed and like a large whale the bow rises up again, holding herself steady for a moment whilst the confused currents around the barge sorts themselves out, then levels out before being taken with the tide on up The Parting.

The Globe Inn is situated on a sharp bend of a very narrow part of the river with steel piling around the outside of the bend. Getting the grain barge around this bend is difficult in normal water, but with the tide flowing fast, the adrenalin pumping, you miss the cold steel of the piling by millimetres! As you speed towards the top of The Parting, where this channel joins the main part of the river again, the tide can be seen racing across from Maisemore, creating a whirlpool effect near to the old Tar Works, now a chemical reclamation plant. As the barge leaves The Parting she is taken across this whirlpool and lay on her side as at great speed she races around the sweep of the bend, too close to the bank for comfort!

Having survived all of that, we are now in the wide reach of the Severn and I steer her into the fastest flow of the tide to gain the extra speed which will get me to Tewkesbury an hour later, [on a good day without the assistance of the tide it is a 4 hour trip from Gloucester]. There is a speed limit of 6 mph on the Severn, but this spring tide is pushing up at some 15 mph now, with large trees, beer kegs, dead animals, etc., having to be pushed out of the way. If I am fortunate I can make Upper Lode Lock at Tewkesbury before the ebb and if my luck holds both top and bottom gates of the lock will be open enabling me to sail through without stopping. This phenomenon is caused by the level of the river being the same top and bottom of the lock and will only last for a few minutes, but will take another 20 minutes off the trip.

One trip I made good time up The Parting from Gloucester and knowing there was a good tide due that morning I waited above the Tar Works for it to arrive. Normally above Maisemore weir there is no bore wave, just the surge of a mass of water racing and rising rapidly towards Ashleworth. That morning as I waited with eyes straining for the tide to appear from around the bend, I was amazed to see a bore wave approaching. Seconds before the wave reached the stern of the barge I increased the engine revs to full ahead and rode the bore until the wave vanished at the top of the first reach.

Of course things didn't always go quite so smoothly. Another trip I locked the laden barge out of Gloucester Lock into a shallow Severn and lost the steerage with the result that the stern of the vessel went across the river and stuck in the mud on the bank. The bow remained in deeper water over towards The Quay wall, but fortunately a spring tide was due an hour later so it was just a question of being patient and wait. *[see photograph on opposite page]*. This trip I had a young chap, Dan, as mate, who had never been on the barge on a spring tide and his eagerness showed as he paced around the stern deck constantly looking at his watch muttering that it was late coming.

The grain barge CHACELEY heads out of Gloucester Lock loaded with 250 tonnes of grain for the mill at Tewkesbury. This is the exact spot where she was stuck across the river shortly before a big tide was due.

*Jon H Talbot*

Dan was first to see the tide as it surged around the bend past Gloucester Lock and as it hit the stern of the barge he screamed out in fear. The stern lifted off the mud with the force of the water and was taken diagonally along The Quay with me struggling to straighten her up. Coming around the top bend I could see an inflatable dinghy with 3 men in it and feared that my barge would sweep into them, but fortunately they had the presence of mind to turn around and race on ahead and by the time I reached that top bend the barge had settled down, steering steadily with the flow.

What about bringing the empty barge back to Gloucester against the tide? We left Tewkesbury one morning calculating that we should be below Westgate Bridge as the spring tide arrived. Unfortunately we were delayed at Upper Lode Lock and midway between Ashleworth and The Parting we met the surging tide as it sped up the river. The force was that strong that it stopped the barge and at one point I feared that we were going to be taken back upstream with the tide! As it was I just had enough power to hold the barge in the current punching against the tide to maintain steerage until the force of the tide receded. My troubles were not over for as I entered The Parting I was informed on the radio by Gloucester Lock Keeper that his depth gauge was showing 5.1m, too high for the barge to get under Westgate Bridge. By now the tide was ebbing and running fast down the narrow channel of The Parting so I instructed the mate to be ready on the stern to throw a rope onto a tree stump as we went around the bend at the Glob Inn. Even with the propeller going full astern we were travelling quite fast around the bend, but with his skill the mate was able to get the eye of the rope over a tree stump and help stop the barge. Thirty minutes later the radio crackled into life again to say that the river had dropped sufficiently for me to get the empty grain barge under Westgate Bridge.

The grain barge TIRLEY goes to the aid of the tug SPEEDWELL which had become stuck in the mud below Gloucester Lock.

*drawing by Chris Witts*

# Stuck in the Mud

During the latter part of the summer the Severn normally experiences very low water levels making it difficult to navigate a loaded barge out of Gloucester Lock and along The Quay. British Waterways are on hand to offer assistance and on this particular day supplied the powerful motor tug SPEEDWELL to tow the loaded grain barge TIRLEY from Gloucester to Ashleworth.

Unfortunately it didn't quite go as planned! The tug locked down from the dock basin first and waited outside the lock for the grain barge to level down. A tow rope was made secure between the two vessels and slowly the tug eased ahead taking the strain on the rope as the skipper of the barge slowly increased the revs to full ahead.

Suddenly there was a loud crack as the tow rope parted, but the TIRLEY had begun to move and her bow began pushing the stern of the tug around. Although the river level was low there is always a vicious current running across the entrance to the lock and it was this that caused the tug to go sideways across the river to become stuck under the new footbridge spanning the Severn from Severn Road to Alney Island.

The grain barge crew tied a rope from the bow to the quay wall and began to drop the stern towards the tug. Then disaster. The barge became stuck in the mud as well! Fortunately the lock keeper realised the predicament they were all in and quickly filled the lock up, then opened fully the bottom paddles which caused all the water in the lock to escape with enough force to lift both vessels off the mud.

Two years after this episode and not long after I had been appointed skipper of the grain barges I became stuck in the river with the TIRLEY for two days at the Upper Parting. Again the powerful motor tug SPEEDWELL was sent to assist me, also with a new skipper, but having spent all of the afternoon of the first day in only towing the barge 500m the tow was abandoned until the following day That day after 3 hours of trying to free the barge off the mud everyone was on the point of giving in and having to face a long wait for the next set of spring tides. Perseverance paid off though, for slowly but surely the SPEEDWELL began to move the TIRLEY through the mud.

The problem of low water levels is added to by large amounts of silt being dumped on the bed of the river each time the spring tides race over the weirs at Gloucester. The reason for the river looking murky at Gloucester is the millions of grains of silt held in suspension in the water as it travels upriver until when the tide ebbs out the silt drops to the bed of the river. It doesn't take much imagination to work out that by multiplying all the silt held in suspension and being carried on the tides above Gloucester twice a day for a few days twice a month that a lot of mud is lying underneath the water! When fresh it is like milk jelly and can be dispersed quite easily, in fact when the barges hit fresh tumps of silt the water would become like cocoa as the mound was broken apart. If left for a few weeks undisturbed though, then it becomes hard and stops the barges from riding over it.

That is why there is only one good method of keeping the river free of all this silt, loaded barges regularly trading on the Severn above Gloucester keeping the channels open by frequently knocking out the mud.

On a good day the loaded grain barges could navigate up the three miles of The Parting from Gloucester to the old tar works at Sandhurst in one hour. Ideally this was achieved when the depth gauge at Gloucester Lock was showing 3.7m, any more and the current coming downstream was too fast to push against, any less an there was the likelihood of getting stuck in the mud. The barges were loaded *down by the head*, that is the bow of the vessels would be about 10cms lower in the water than the stern. Then if a mound of hidden mud was struck and the skipper of the barge was able to get the bow over it, then the rest of the craft would follow. If the barge was loaded *by the stern*, the bow may get over the tump of mud, but the chances are the hull would stick on it towards the stern, causing the vessel to pivot and become jammed across the river.

Getting jammed across the river is the worst scenario of becoming stuck in the mud. The barge acts as a dam holding back the water running downstream and usually requires the assistance of other vessels to free the stricken vessel. During the 1950s a tanker barge became stuck this way and whilst being helped by another tanker barge that became stuck too. A third barge also became stuck whilst trying to assist the first two! All three barges had to wait a week for the arrival of a set of spring tides to assist them in getting free from their predicament.

The grain barges TIRLEY and CHACELEY were built for carrying coal on the River Trent, therefore they did not handle too well on the Severn during low water levels and when there was a significant amount of freshwater running down the river. With their bluff bow and low powered engines they struggled through the silt, causing frustration to the private small craft that would form a queue behind the barge as it moved so slowly up The Parting.

About 50m below the old tar works in the East Channel of The Parting three tumps of mud would regularly appear. If the barge struggled over the first two then it was guaranteed that the third would stop the vessel. Over a period of weeks this hump would gradually grow across the river to hold the barge up for at least an hour as it tried to find a way over it. The secret was patience, but I'm afraid that was hard to achieve! In frustration the skipper would drop his barge astern of the tump then make a fast run at it with the hope of either breaking the mud apart or to ride over it. The best way would be to get stuck on the tump of mud then wait patiently as the current scoured a hole under the barge, move forward and wait again. Unfortunately this could take hours, time which barge skippers didn't have, knowing that the flour mill was desperate for your cargo.

Having passed these three notoriously bad tumps of mud fresh problems lie ahead. Where the East Channel joins again with the West Channel it is only a narrow channel out of The Parting. But like Gloucester Lock the current is strong as it sweeps across the entrance, flowing fast down to Maisemore Weir. I was taking the loaded TIRLEY out of The Parting one morning and although I had the wheel hard to starboard to make the slight right turn to follow the channel around the river the bow was not responding. The current became master and began taking the TIRLEY astern back down the West Channel towards the weir. This was during low summer level and with the little Gardner 6LX engine working at full revs still she kept going astern. There was nothing myself or the mate could do, only watch as nature worked at her worst against us. The weir was getting closer, but fortunately the propeller began to grip and we slowly made our way back out of the West Channel and into deeper water. Every trip after that episode I treated that part of The Parting with the utmost respect!

It would appear that the Severn at Gloucester is still suffering from lack of attention. Certainly towards the end of my time on the grain barges the river was in desperate need of help, the relevant authorities instead of engaging in a concerted effort to make it good again would each dabble a little and make no progress. To my horror on my last few trips down the river with the empty grain barges I became stuck twice on the bend above Black Bridge, the railway bridge about one mile above Gloucester Lock. With all the water ballast emptied out and ropes ashore to winch ourselves off the mud we still remained stuck. Again we had to seek assistance from British Waterways who this time sent up the powerful hopper barge TEME to help us.

The Severn Navigation Restoration Trust have recently released a report on the state of the river and says that urgent action is needed to save the Severn. One of the possible problems of low water levels in the summer is the increase in the amount of water abstracted each year by the various water authorities. It further states that the Severn is a river in crisis and unless urgent action is taken it could suffer terminal damage. The deterioration of the river has been happening for years almost unnoticed and unless something radical is done soon who knows what the Severn will be looking like in fifty years time, if indeed the river is still flowing then!

Motor barge SEVERN INDUSTRY [left] with dumb barges at Avonmouth Docks.
The SEVERN INDUSTRY is now the home of Mike May at Stonebench [pg 26]
*Chris Witts*

Steam tug MAYFLOWER. Built in 1861 for use on the River Severn. This tug is
now preserved as a working exhibit at Bristol Docks.
*Chris Witts*

# Fishing
# the
# Lower Severn

Anything to do with the Severn below Gloucester is hard work, surfing, handling a barge, or even fishing. Mention fishing and it conjures up thoughts of an angler sitting sedately on the bank with rod and line. Not so the men who fish for salmon, out in all weathers, thigh deep in tidal water using all the energy they can muster to catch that elusive fish.

Although elvermen and those who fish for eels do not have to stand in the waters of the Severn, they are fishing at night in some inhospitable places. The difference between these men and the rod and line angler seen farther up the river, is that the angler will return his catch to the Severn, whereas a good salmon, buckets of elvers and several eels will reap rich rewards.

## Salmon

From the sea salmon enter the Severn for spawning far up in the shallow and gravel parts of the river. In the upper estuary salmon will swim close to the surface with their backs out of the water and are at risk of becoming grounded on the gently shelving sands of the river and as the tide ebbs they remain stranded on the sand to the mercy of the numerous gulls flying overhead in search of food. Due to the Severn being a shallow river it became necessary in the mid 19th century to build several weirs between Gloucester and Stourport to artificially raise the level of the river. To get to their breeding grounds high up the River Severn the salmon somehow have to overcome the obstacles of these weirs, but having had the stamina to swim all this way from the sea they are not going to let it stop them from getting to their breeding grounds! Summing up all their energy they swim hard and fast towards the weir, then leap into the air to land back in the water topside of the obstruction., but when the level of the river is low special *salmon shutes* have been built on the weirs to assist the fish to jump them. Like a lot of British rivers, stocks of salmon are depleting in the Severn which is giving cause for concern amongst the various nature and environmental bodies.

Should our salmon get to the breeding grounds to spawn, the eggs when hatched are 5mm in diameter and known as *alevins*, but due to being imperfectly developed they carry in their abdomen a large stock of food yolk which will give nourishment during the first few weeks of their life. It is not until the fry are two months old that they begin to feed and adopt the barred colours, normal for this *parr* stage of their life.

The young fry remain in the freshwater of the upper reaches of the Severn for at least two years, by which time they have lost the parr markings and change to the silvery hue so characteristic of our salmon. At this stage they are only 10cm long and referred to as *smolt* and are ready for the long journey back to the sea.

They could after only two years at sea return to spawn again in the freshwater of the river, but normally remain in the ocean for several years. It is not until they have reached the age of four years that they can be called salmon, before this the name *grilse* is given to them, or on the Severn, *botchers*.

Salmon has always been a delicacy of our dining tables commanding high prices at the fish market. Non better than the fresh run salmon with silvery hue and plenty of red flesh full of fat, but not so nice though after they have been breeding, when they become so thin with their colour changing to a dull grey or brown. Fish that have travelled upriver for spawning often weigh as much as 4 kilos, but after, have shrunk in size and now only weigh 2 kilos!

Traditionally salmon have been caught on the Severn between the Severn Suspension Bridge and Longney by men and their lave nets. Little has changed with this method of catching salmon apart

Deryck Huby 'cowering' with his lave net waiting for that elusive salmon

*Dave Hawkins*

Deryck with a salmon in the lave net

*Dave Hawkins*

from now the high cost of the annual licence fee and a close season from the 1st of September until the 30th May. A lave net is timber framed with the favourite wood being ash or hazel nut made into different parts known as the *handstaff*, the *shoulder*, the *yoke board*, the *rimes*, the *toe*, the *head-line*, the *bosom* and the *wings*. When assembled the lave net forms a Y with netting and can be folded up to be carried on the fisherman's shoulder. Part of the licence agreement is that on the *yoke board* there must be fitted a yellow tag with the licensee's number on it.

No date can be given as to when the lave net first appeared on the Severn, but they were certainly in use in the 17th century as John Smyth of Nibley makes mention of them in his writings of that period.

The art of lave net fishing is passed on from generation to generation with each man knowing his area of the river intimately. As the seasons change so do the sandbanks, vital for the fishermen's existence. A spell of high freshwater coming down into the estuary from the upper reaches can wash away sandbanks, testing their patience as he waits for the next set of spring tides to hopefully replace them as they were. All this freshwater coming down river isn't liked by the salmon either, they will not swim into the dirty water, but wait farther down the estuary until the water becomes clear again. Salmon are caught with the lave net on the ebbing tide and as they realise that they are in shallow water above the sandbanks will swim with the ebb searching for deeper water unaware of the keen eyed fisherman waiting patiently to catch it!

Not only keen eyes, but physical stamina is demanded of the men out in the river with their lave nets, for on seeing the wash from a salmon he must run through the water to get ahead of the fish. He flicks the lave net from his shoulder into the water with the toe resting on the river bed with seconds to spare as the salmon swims towards the net. Deftly the net is raised from the river at precisely the right time giving great satisfaction to the fisherman as he examines his catch.

The lave net with the fish still in it is driven into the sand whilst the fisherman kills the salmon with a blow between the eyes using a stout truncheon called a *knocker*. This is not as cruel as it sounds for a salmon will die if it is out of the water for a few minutes and even putting it back into the water whilst alive will not revive it.

Not so many years ago lave net fishing was very common on the Severn with great rivalry amongst the hundreds of men fishing for salmon this way, but not any more. Only a few are still licensed to use lave nets, Ken Hill, or as he is known locally Dasher, is one of them. Living at Frampton on Severn he can remember the time when there were an abundance of salmon in the river, but over the last few years numbers caught has decreased rapidly, 1998 being his worst season when he caught not one! During the early part of the following year he did see some going through to spawn upriver during the close season, "Hopefully", he said, " A sign that it will be a better season than last!".

Along the banks of the estuary as far up the river as Newnham can be seen during the season hundreds of wicker baskets. Known as putchers, as many as three hundred can be fixed to stakes running at right angles from the bank into the river. The putchers are 1.8m long and have a mouth of 0.8m wide tapering to 50mm are fixed in tiers normally three high with the putcher mouth facing upstream, completely covered by the tide at high water. As the tide ebbs any unsuspecting salmon will swim into the putcher, caught in the trap, for with its inability to swim backwards will die within minutes of being left high and dry. Although the putchers are inspected after each tide for any salmon that may be caught in them, only a very small percentage of fish get trapped this way. The success of the putcher is dependent on the tide, as it ebbs out with the hedging steering the salmon into the putchers, but then, no two tides are alike!

Deryck Huby and his colleague Donald Riddle had their own salmon fishing ground at Hayward Rock, some distance downstream from Berkeley Power Station. Sadly they have not fished here for a season and now this area will likely fall foul of the tides and slowly disappear into the mud. Their season began in February, not fishing, but cutting hazel, using the flexible stems in major repairs to the hedging out in the Severn. They had 300m of hedging to maintain, requiring a daily inspection to check that the vicious tides weren't causing too much damage. Then in March they would harvest willow to make new putchers. The willow would be cut, bundled and tied securely, left to dry for two to three weeks before being woven in the traditional method of basket weaving. Sadly putchers are not made by this way now, instead they are constructed with metal, for ease of maintenance and longer life. Age creeps upon us all, the reason these two true Severnsiders had to give up this way of life, sadly with no one younger wishing to follow in their footsteps. They can remember though, the one that didn't get away, a whopping 16 kilos!

Another wicker basket similar in shape to the putcher, but much larger is the putt, more complicated in construction, they measure 1.8m in diameter and 4.3m in length with three separate sections called, *kype, butt* and *forewheel* and like the putchers they are positioned with their mouths facing upstream to catch the salmon on the ebb. Deryck and Donald used to have 20 putts to look after, but found in latter years that there was so much plastic rubbish floating in the Severn Estuary that instead of finding fish in them would discover the putts full of rubbish. So they decided in 1985 to remove the putts and to concentrate on the putchers and lave net.

Like the lave net, putchers and putts have been in use for many centuries, but were often criticised in Parliament, especially during the 19th century, where various acts were passed in an endeavour to stop their use. Each putcher and putt had to be licensed to catch salmon, continuing to the present day where it is becoming increasingly difficult to obtain the necessary licence. During the close season the putchers must be removed from the weirs, but due to their large size putts may be left in the river and to prevent salmon entering the putt two stout withy rods are driven crossways through the mouth.

Very few putchers and putts are used today to catch salmon, only five sites on the west bank between Slime Road and Newnham on Severn and none on the east bank, but the remains of many may still be seen along the estuary. During a pleasant walk along the shoreline from Littleton to the majestic Severn Suspension Bridge can be seen a derelict weir looking forlorn and abandoned in the black mud of he Severn.

Two methods of catching salmon with nets were in use in the

Derek Huby checking his putchers for salmon.

*Dave Hawkins*

Putchers stored ashore and lave net folded, the end of the season for Deryck.

*Chris Witts*

river below Gloucester. The stop net, was in use on the broad lower reaches of the river where the tide runs fierce through the channel was used with craft known as stopping-boats. Stopping boats were a purpose built sturdy craft 6.7m long and crewed by one man using the sculling method to propel it through the shallow water together with the net of 9.2m long and held taut between two heavy wooden arms in a V shape over the side of the boat. The little hamlet of Gatcombe is not only famous for its visit by Sir Francis Drake, but also for its stopping-boats, some still to be seen lying on the bank alongside the main Gloucester to South Wales railway line. This form of fishing for salmon has always been recognised as the most dangerous where out in the fierce tides the boats develop a heavy list to one side and despite the strength and skill of the boatman the craft can turn over. If he is lucky he will jump out of the boat before it turns over, hopefully retrieving his fishing gear a mile or more upstream. Within the last fifty years two out of the eight stopping-boat men have been drowned as their boats have gone over.

Farther upriver the long net is still in use for catching salmon with the net 182m in length and requiring four men to work it. This method is now banned in the Severn upstream of Madam Pool at Elmore, but at one time was a common sight between Ashleworth and Apperley until the increase in motor barge traffic spoilt it for the fishermen. Sadly few now fish for salmon below Gloucester with the long net. It is hardly profitable when taking the cost of the licence into consideration and the decline in salmon in the Severn. Those who do still fish with this old traditional method only do it part-time and as a hobby. Because of the low price that salmon now fetch in the markets any fish caught tends to be eaten by the fishermen or given away to friends. Frequently new rules are introduced by the licensing authority and it is thought amongst today's fishermen that the days of catching salmon on the Severn with nets may be numbered.

Like the salmon, fishing for this magnificent fish is in decline on the Severn below Gloucester, the number of licensees issued for 1998 prove this!

1998 figures reveal that there were a total of 31 licenses issued for fishing for salmon below Gloucester and that as of 1999 the season will be from the 1st June until the 31st August. The current cost of the licence for lave net fishing is £42, but those who fish with nets have to pay £200, whilst putchers are charged at £55 per fifty.

When salmon are caught farther upriver it is classed as game fishing and traditionally the sport of rich landowners and aristocrats. Nowadays this sport is well within reach of most anglers. They are caught using that well proven method of fly fishing, with a soft and whippy rod, line and a feathered hook known as an *artificial fly*. Fishing for salmon with this method is totally different to that used down the lower reaches of the Severn, suffice to say it can be quite relaxing sitting on the bank of the Severn at Bewdley watching a fly fisherman out in the river casting his line to lure the elusive salmon to the fly.

Why does the salmon take the bait of the artificial fly upriver when in fresh water this fish ceased feeding as they entered the river? No one knows, for it remains one of life's mysteries!

A fisherman and his lave net
*drawing by Chris Witts*

# Elvers

During the dark nights of the third week of February a strange sight will greet a visitor to the banks of the River Severn below Gloucester. The river is lit with hundreds of lights along both banks, each with someone keenly waiting for the first spring tide of the season.

Who are these people who must be mad to wait around on a cold winters night in inhospitable surroundings? They are elvermen, men who annually take their strange looking nets to the river in the hope of securing a large catch of translucent, worm looking fish. Elvers, for centuries a local delicacy, once sold in pint mugs around the city streets, cooked alive by housewives' in a frying pan together with the fat from a nice piece of bacon.

Now they are far too expensive for the locals to buy, even the traditional elver eating contest at Frampton on Severn had to be scrapped. A day where men and women would sit at long tables with a large plate of elvers in front of them, the winner being the one who could eat the most in the shortest time! It is nothing new for a contestant to swallow a pound of elvers in 37 seconds. Recognised as being an aphrodisiac, would the participating contestants indulge in amorous activities, even with the bloated state of their stomachs! Tons of elvers are still being caught each year, but not for the British markets, as it all became very commercial a number of years ago when elver stations began buying all fish caught and selling them on to foreign buyers for breeding purposes. In actual fact back in 1908 four million elvers were exported to Germany for stocking their rivers, supplied by the first elver station in the county, located then at the Anchor Inn, Epney.

There is much competition amongst elvermen to secure the best spot on the bank to fish for elvers and a few weeks before the start of the season they can be seen staking a claim to their tump by tying plastic buckets in trees. Some may have several tumps marked along the river, several miles apart. Woe betide anyone who should dare to fish on someone else's tump! It is now so competitive that besides the annual licence fee of £20 required to fish for elvers, farmers are charging fees to the elvermen for the privilege of being on their land.

The common eel found in our rivers breed two thousand miles away in the Atlantic Ocean, south east of Bermuda in the Sargasso Sea. Larvae is hatched from the eels in the tropical weed bed before beginning the long three year journey back to the Bristol Channel. In the New Year the larvae is entering the Bristol Channel and changing into small transparent creatures about 7.5cm long. They remain here for about a month whilst undergoing a change in behaviour. Not liking bright light they stay in deep water and try to avoid contact with each other. The elver has also to change from a salt water fish to a fresh water one, besides having to wait for the water temperature to rise in the estuary.

By late February the time is right for countless thousands of elvers to congregate in large shoals and begin their journey into fresher water, swimming at night on the big tides, guided upstream by the banks in the ever narrowing river. Having travelled all this way, they spend between eight and twelve years in the fresh waters of the river growing into mature eels before travelling back down the Severn during the autumn to begin the long journey back across the Atlantic to their breeding grounds, never to return to our shores again. Elvers may be portrayed as innocent little creatures trying to survive long enough to make their journey back upriver to where their parents left a few years previously, but don't feel too sorry for them. They are cannibals. Fill a tank of water full of elvers and years later there will be left just one well fed eel!

Elvers are caught on the Severn between Sharpness and Upper Lode weir at Tewkesbury with the season lasting from the end of February until the middle of May and can only be caught from the bank as it is illegal to catch them from a boat out in the river. There is no close season now, whereby between certain dates it is illegal to fish for elvers. In 1935 the Government removed a close season and classed elvers, together with whitebait, as the only fish fry which may be fished for food at any time of the year. There has been a worry for many centuries that elvers are being over fished and their numbers are dwindling. In 1558 at the beginning of the reign of Elizabeth I until the year of 1778 a complete ban was enforced on the fishing of elvers in British rivers. This ban was then lifted, but they could only be caught for eating and not for selling, although records show that in Gloucestershire they were being sold for two pence a pound! In 1876 the Elver Fishing Act was introduced which did include a close season.

Although a few are caught during the day, it is on the spring tides at night that elvers are fished, just as the tide turns and beginning to ebb out. As with all good and experienced fishermen, elvermen keep their knowledge of knowing where the elvers will be on subsequent tides to themselves. For example it would be a waste of time going to fish for elvers above Gloucester if the tide at Sharpness was less than 8 metres in height, the incoming flow would not rise above Maisemore and Llanthony weirs.

Traditionally elvermen would make their own nets for catching elvers, but now they can be purchased ready made from the elver stations! They are 1m long by 0.6m wide and 0.5m deep with a framework made of willow at the end of a 1.5m pole, [now ready made elver net frames are made of aluminium]. Whether the framework is made of traditional willow or the modern aluminium, all are covered with a form of cheesecloth, tightly stretched across the frame. Armed with net, bucket and trays hundreds of men set off for their tumps, many carrying their nets lashed to the roof of their cars. Tilley lamps are lit and then they wait for the cry of "Flood oh" as the tide approaches, with a further wait of about an hour for the tide to turn before flashing their lights momentarily in the water hoping to see swarms of silvery, wriggling elvers swimming against the ebb. As the tide races in thousands of elvers are swimming out in the middle of the river going with the flow, but when the tide begins to ebb they continue to swim upriver, but choose to take the route with the least resistance, that is swimming against the current close into the bank. The nets are dipped in the river, lifted out and the catch tipped into the bucket, repeated over and over again for two hours or more. Each lift of the net is termed a *shutt* and the amount of the catch is measured in pints. With these strange translucent creatures squirming to escape up the side of the bucket a few inches of foam is formed giving the appearance of a freshly drawn pint of beer. The elvers must not remain in the bucket for too long for fear of damaging them, so are regularly,

A wriggling mass of elvers
*Gloucester Folk Museum*

A man and his catch of elvers
*sketched from photograph*

with care, placed on the hesian base of the numerous trays which accompany each elverman.

Should there not be many elvers showing that tide the elvermen will position his net in the river, pegged to the bank with two sticks and then sit back and wait for any stray elvers to swim into and remain in the net, this is called *tealing*. Sometimes the elvers will drop back with the ebb tide and the net has to be turned to face upstream, this is known as *sagging*.

Finally after a long night on the river bank the catch is taken to an elver station where they are weighed and checked before each elverman receives a handsome reward for his hard and sometimes difficult work.

Towards the end of the season the elvers develop small bones which has the effect of making them look black and unpleasant to eat, thus the time for the elver season to finish for another year.

The annual elver licence operates from the 1st of April in the current year until the 31st March of the following, it costs £20 and in 1998 a total of 1,321 were issued.

> There was a young elver called Freddie
> Who said to himself "I'm not ready
> To help fill the tum
> Of an elverer's mum"
> So he dodged elver nets - clever Freddie

written by Betty Dyer
of Highnam W.I.,Gloucester
[Sept 1998]

# Eels

Should our wriggly little elver be so lucky to swim past all those men with their strange shaped nets on the lower reaches of the Severn they may stand a chance of growing into another rare delicacy, the eel.

Swimming against the current, elvers battle their way up-river as far as the upper reaches of the river, some staying in the Severn, others swimming into tributaries such as the River Teme. Here for the next four years or longer they develop into the *yellow eel* or *guelps* with an attractive yellow and green colour on their undersides. Remaining on the bottom of the rivers they feed on the freshwater food of crayfish, snails, fish eggs and tadpoles. Several years later when fully mature they have lost their appetite to eat and turn into a blue black colour with a white underside and are now known as *silver eels* or *vawsen*. They have also undergone a physical change to prepare them for a change from fresh water into salt water and the depths they will have to face in the Atlantic. The body of the eel is cylindrical and elongated with the single dorsal fin merging with the tail and the anal fin on the underside. It has a small head with small teeth in the mouth and behind the gill openings is a single pair of fins. To the angler they are a nuisance who are not really interested in catching eels and therefore will spend a lot of time trying to avoid them.

Now as the dark winter nights approach they prepare themselves for the long return journey back down the Severn, out into the Bristol Channel and across the Atlantic Ocean to the Sargasso Sea. That is if they can pass more men waiting to catch them as they approach Gloucester, the favourite and best place to catch eels.

It remains one of our mysteries why during the dark nights of autumn between the last and first quarter of the moon and normally between sunset and midnight these fully mature eels should migrate *en masse* down the Severn. Should the river have some fresh water flowing down, muddy and the weather stormy, then there will be an abundance of eels swimming down with the cur-

# Gloucester Wing Net

Netsman would go out in punt, lift cod, empty them and retie to continue fishing

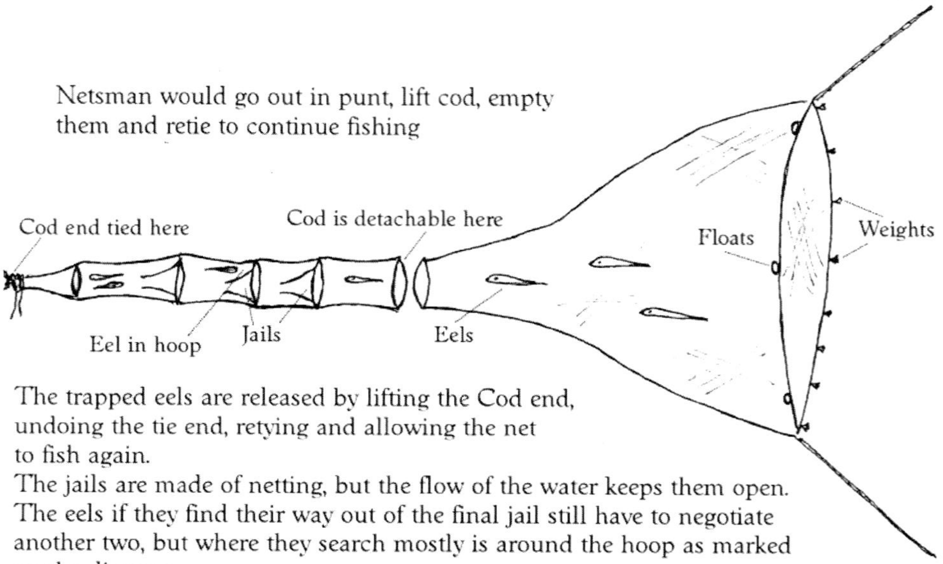

Cod end tied here

Cod is detachable here

Eel in hoop

Jails

Eels

The trapped eels are released by lifting the Cod end, undoing the tie end, retying and allowing the net to fish again.
The jails are made of netting, but the flow of the water keeps them open. The eels if they find their way out of the final jail still have to negotiate another two, but where they search mostly is around the hoop as marked on the diagram

Floats

Weights

Moorings

*diagram by Dave Hawkins*

Fig. 4

# Three Types of Putcheon
# Used for Catching Eels

Old Type
Made of willow or hazel

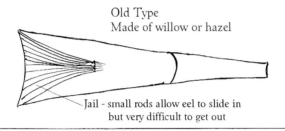

Jail - small rods allow eel to slide in
but very difficult to get out

Locally Made Modern Type
Metal frame covered in wire mesh

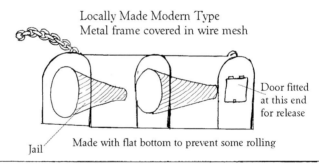

Door fitted
at this end
for release

Jail    Made with flat bottom to prevent some rolling

Plastic Type

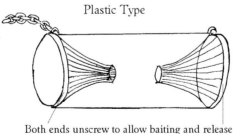

Both ends unscrew to allow baiting and release

Fig. 5

*diagram by Dave Hawkins*

rent. Many fishermen believe that the male eel migrates down river a little earlier than the female and will wait a mile or so upstream of Gloucester until they meet again.

One method of catching eels was by use of a spear, but now prohibited. These had a wrought iron head with three to nine flat spines with serrated edges with the tines having blunt ends with a little amount of spring in them. The spear was mounted on an ash handle about 6.1m or more in length. To catch the eels the spear was plunged vertically into mud under the water with the eel becoming wedged between the tines.

Two Acts of Parliament were introduced in the early part of the twentieth century which gave reference to the fishing of eels. The first in 1911 made it law that licenses were required to fish for freshwater fish of any kind, which included eels. No licenses were issued for eel spears, but their unlicensed use was deemed illegal.

Then in 1923 another Act prohibited the use of spears for catching freshwater fish, but exempted eels! But as this new Act did not repeal the 1911 Act then eel spears remained illegal on the Severn.

Today the eels are fished commercially by netting them in large numbers during their brief autumn migration to the sea. The majority of the annual catch will be netted on about six nights of this period. On average a single net catch can be up to 69 kilos of eels and in 1959 it is recorded that from one net a total catch of 1 tonne of eels was made! Figures that are not likely to be repeated, for like the salmon, eels are sadly in decline.

Those fishing for eels for commercial gain must have a licence and inform the Environment Agency of how many eels they have taken from the Severn. A lot of these eels caught for commercial use will find their way to the continental fish markets of Holland, Germany and Scandinavia, with some going to the London jellied eel markets.

Nets used for eel fishing are made in size to suit the particular part of the river they are being used in. [*Fig 4*] A long tapering sleeve with a wide mouth is flanked by wings with the sleeve supported at regular intervals by cane or iron hoops with the net fixed to these hoops. Within the sleeve of the net is a couple of cone shaped non-return valves held tight by strings when the net is in use. At the end of the net in which the eel is caught is called the *cod end*. Eel nets are used in conjunction with the Severn punt and during the autumn these punts can be seen tied to the bank of the river, vulnerable though, to the spring tides as they sweep upriver filling the craft with water. It only takes a few weeks of neglect on the part of the punt owner before the mud claims the punt and buries it under the silt!

During one night in the October of 1977 a small inshore trawler, the HYLANDER, went out into the Severn at Sandhurst to trawl for eels in the middle of the river. It was an experiment which didn't have a lot of success, not only was the catch poor, the net became entangled in the propeller requiring divers to be sent for to go down and cut away the net. Trawling for eels with this method had its critics, other fishermen were concerned that a precedent could be set and in following years would see not one, but several boats fishing for eels this way. As it happened the experiment was not repeated.

Basket traps are also used for catching eels, now constructed of galvanised iron wire, the *putcheon*, about 1m in length with a mouth 25cms wide and the *weel* 3.5m long with an opening of 40cms. [*Fig 5*] Both are of similar shape, wide mouth, bellied in the centre, then tapering to a small opening at the other end. Each trap is then fitted with a couple of constricted throats of canes towards the narrow end. A piece of rabbit or lamprey is then put in the narrow end to act as bait, finally stopped with turf or rag before the trap is tied to the bank and weighed down with stones. Depending where the traps are located dictates how they are laid in the river, above Gloucester the traps mouth faces upstream, below the mouth faces either way so as to catch the eels moving up and down with the tides.

Finally one simple, but ingenious way of catching eels is *putting* or *bobbing*. A 6.1m length of twine has freshly dug earthworms threaded on to it, the twine is then coiled into small loops. This mass of coils is fixed to another line and with lead weights, dangled in the river waiting for an eel to take the bait and become entangled in the coils. Eel men say this form of fishing is no longer practised, finishing during the 1940's

A favourite haunt of eel during the daytime is a hole in the bank. Then a method known as *sniggling* was employed to tempt the resting eel to take the bait. Basically a stout needle with a fresh worm was whipped onto a length of twine then fixed onto a stick. The *sniggle*, as it is now called, was pushed as far as possible into the hole to wait for the eel to take the bait. Having allowed time for the eel to swallow the worm the fisherman pulls on the twine which forces the needle across the gullet. The eel would resist every effort to be captured and only after becoming exhausted was it pulled from the hole. It will be difficult to find a fisherman who has seen this form of catching eels practised as it is one of those old traditions that finished a long time ago.

It was traditional that the Severnside dweller kept an eel box or trunk floating in the river at the bottom of the garden. Freshly caught eels could be kept in these boxes alive until ready for market or required for eating. Now wire cages are used which will sink and be hidden to prevent theft.

Once the eel has left the Severn no one is absolutely sure if they do return back to the Sargasso Sea, for no adult eel has been caught in this area! We can only guess that spawning takes place some 100 to 200m down below the surface of the sea at a winter temperature of 20C. Sadly though, that is the last we see of them for they are gone, gone for good never to return to our shores again.

# The Water Bailiff

Someone has to police the river to check that angler, elvermen and salmon fishermen have the correct licence to fish the river, that someone is the water bailiff. A small team of men who regularly patrol the river checking licences and occasionally catching the poacher.

The water bailiff is the Law Enforcement Officer employed by the Environment Agency as their Fisheries Officer and is someone who is first and foremost a nature lover. Usually a fisherman themselves they know the river better than most and will gladly give welcome advice to anyone who requires it. The Law Enforcement Officer for the Lower Severn region covers both banks of the river from Worcester down to where the estuary joins the Bristol Channel.

With the vast numbers of elver licences issued each year and the fierce competition amongst elvermen, this has to be the busiest time of the year for the bailiff. The worry at present is that some nasty incidents have occurred between elvermen and the authorities resulting in the need for the water bailiff to summon help from the police. The boom time for elvermen may be coming to an end, perhaps then peace will be restored on the river and local inhabitants may enjoy a pint of elvers at a realistic price.

# My Favourite Recipes

## A Plate of Elvers

*Pint of Elvers*
*Bacon Fat*
*Two Eggs*
*Gammon*
*Salt*
*Vinegar*
*Black Pepper*

Heat the bacon fat in a large frying pan, smack in the elvers then break the eggs over them. Mix well together and cook for about ten minutes

Serve on a warm plate with a nice piece of choice gammon. Sprinkle on vinegar, salt and black pepper.
Eat with plenty of fresh bread and butter.

*Recipe courtesy of Dasher.*

## Cooking an Eel

*Eel*
*Cooking Oil*
*Flour*
*Fresh Salad*
*Salt*
*Vinegar*

The eel has to be skinned, [hard, even for the expert, so please seek help!]. Then it is chopped into 2cm thick steaks and covered in flour. Warm oil in large frying pan, gently place in eel steaks and fry for about 5 minutes until golden brown.
Served with salad and fresh bread they make a crispy and succulent dish.

# Conclusion

Many rivers produce bores of various magnitudes, there is even one more mighty than our own Severn Bore.

Faraway on the Qiantang River in Eastern China, where for many centuries their bore has brought fear to those who live close to the river, a solid wall of water moves up the estuary into the river, making it the worlds largest bore. So awesome a spectacle that the Chinese call it the Silver Dragon, so terrifying that in the 12th century suicidal surfers would ride it in a sacrificial attempt to placate the dragon.

At Hangzhou at the time of the full moon a strong current flows from the Pacific into the trumpet shaped river creating a bore which will almost reach 6m where in past years this great mass of water has wreaked havoc in the countryside killing many thousands of people.

Four intrepid surfers from England, Stuart Matthews, Fred Larkham, Andy Long and John Biddle decided they would like to attempt to surf the Qiantang bore as until recently outsiders had been refused permission by the Chinese to ride the wave. Our four adventurers arrived in China during the autumn period of a full moon which has a special significance for the Chinese, romance!

Stuart would ride the bore, with the others in two inflatable back-up boats and having seen the huge wave the previous day decided to find a more suitable location a little further upriver. They had seen large jack-up rigs and barges tossed around by the bore as they lay at anchor and considered it too dangerous to surf in this part of the river.

That day as they prepared themselves for their adventure, a quarter of a million Chinese people came on their annual pilgrimage to the river to pay homage to the dragon. Moving twice as fast as the Severn Bore, Stuart waited anxiously on his board as the high wave fast approached, soon it was with him and he was up and going with the bore. Exhilarated he managed to surf for eleven seconds, long enough to claim that he rode the Qiantang bore.

Will this be the river that will break Dave Lawson's world record? Will it be Dave Lawson himself who would dearly like someone to sponsor him to go out to China to try for the record on the Qiantang River. Only time will tell.

Only time will tell whether man is ingenious enough to utilise the potential of the power of the Severn, whether for energy, transport or other uses. I certainly hope he doesn't destroy one of Britain's finest natural phenomenon's, the Mighty Severn Bore.

# Boring Facts on the Bore

Bores occur during each month of the year on the spring tides, but the largest are near an equinox, which are in February, March, April, August, September and October.

Observe the bore as it reaches its peak one to three days after a new and full moon.

Rational thinking will let you know if a bore is coming even if you only know the time of high water at Sharpness, for bores always occur between 7am and 7 noon, 7pm and midnight, with the largest between 9am and 11am, 9pm and 11pm. [All times GMT].

Even the height of the bore will vary, with 1m classed as good and 3m is excellent. It will be higher at the bank than in mid-stream and higher still on the outer bank of a bend.

Sadly the bore passes by you very quickly, but it takes between 2hrs.10mins and 2hrs.35mins to travel the 21 miles from Awre to Gloucester.

# Bibliography

Conway-Jones H
   *Working Life on Severn & Canal [1990]*
Gloucestershire Newspapers Ltd
   *The Citizen*
Moriarty C
   *Eels, a natural & unnatural history [1978]*
Neufville Taylor J
   *Fishing on the Lower Severn*
Rowbotham F
   *The Severn Bore [1964]*
Torbett H
   *The Handbook for Fishermen [1964]*
Waters B
   *Severn Tide [1955]*

# Acknowledgements

My thanks to Jo Meredith of Beddows Bookshop, Gloucester who first put the idea in my head; the staff of Gloucester Folk Museum; Dave Lawson & Tomo Wright, the Severn surfers, plus Mike May who lives on the bore; Dave Hawkins and Dasher, both knowledgeable on fishing the lower Severn, and the very patient Joan Allen of the Environment Agency; Patricia Larkham for supplying good bore photographs.

My thanks also to those authors, living and dead, whose work I consulted to help me write this book; to my daughter-in-law Nicki, who designed the book cover and chapter drawings. Finally, last, but not least my wife Carol, for putting up with me whilst involved in this book from start to finish.

Chris Witts

# Gazetteer - The Lower Severn

**Arlingham**
Located in a 9 mile loop of the Severn, once an important prehistoric river crossing to Newnham.

**Awre**
Narrow lanes from the A48 reach this village with its unspoilt 13th century church.

**Bullo Pill**
Once a thriving little port, now lying disused apart from a view private yachts.

**Elmore**
Orchards and watermeadows adorn this area.

**Epney**
Famous for the first elver station on the Severn.

**Frampton on Severn**
Only 8 miles south-west of Gloucester, the village boasts as having one of the largest village greens in England.

**Fretherne**
An unusual Victorian church dominates the skyline when viewed from the Severn.

**Gatcombe**
The hamlet and river divided by the Gloucester to Cardiff railway line.

**Gloucester**
An ancient Roman city established in 43AD has one of England's finest cathedrals. In the 16th century Queen Elizabeth I granted port status to the city.

**Hempsted**
A pretty village only a few miles from Gloucester with its church of St Swithin rebuilt in 1467. A different story though whilst walking along the river bank, the path runs alongside the council tip!